TROUPER

The True Adventures of a Blind Raccoon

The Beginning

by Kyle L. Miller

Jungle House Publications

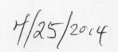

Dedicated to wildlife rehabilitators, who donate their personal time and resources to rescue, rehabilitate and release back to their natural habitats injured, sick and orphaned animals.

Special thanks go to C.R.O.W., the Clinic for the Rehabilitation of Wildlife, on Sanibel Island, FL for the opportunity to photograph an eight-week-old orphan raccoon that was raised and later released into its natural environment.

Text Copyright © 2012 Kyle L. Miller • Photography © 2012 by Kyle L. Miller

Photo Credit: pages 8 and 20, by permission of Dorothy J. Lee

ISBN: 13: 978-0-9769332-5-0

Library of Congress Control Number: 2011919873

Cover and interior design by Sandy Knowles

Summary: A true story about a severely injured baby raccoon named Trouper, that recovered, but was left blind, physically disabled, and became an animal ambassador for wildlife educational purposes.

Juvenile Non-fiction for ages 5 to 8.

Other books by Kyle L. Miller:
DILLO — A Baby Armadillo's Adventure on Sanibel Island ISBN: 978-0-9769332-0-5
Snowy Pea and the Ghost Crab ISBN: 978-0-9769332-3-6

Send all inquiries to:

Kyle L. Miller
Jungle House Publications
736 Cardium St. • Sanibel Island, FL 33957
(239) 472-0599
junglehousepub@yahoo.com • junglehousepublications.com

~ A Note to Parents ~

This is the first in a series of wildlife storybooks for children titled, *Trouper — The True Adventures of a Blind Raccoon*. The series chronicles Trouper's experiences and includes photographs that portray the life of a unique raccoon and his caretaker, Dorothy Lee, and their positive influence on children and families.

Trouper is a survivor of animal cruelty. At eight weeks of age he suffered brain damage after being hit on the head with a golf club. As of April, 2011 he was two years old. He *cannot* see, feed himself, smell, climb, use his hands to pick up things, or defend himself. He *can* hear, eat when hand fed, walk, stand on his back legs, and feel with his feet, whiskers and body. He is not like any other raccoon.

While Trouper is a docile animal, most raccoons are very naughty and destructive, and can even be dangerous. As a result, both Dorothy Lee (Miss Dot) and author Kyle Miller recommend **not** having a raccoon as a pet. In fact, it is against the law to have a raccoon as a pet in Florida unless you have a permit from the Florida Fish and Wildlife Commission.

Because Trouper cannot be released into the wild, he has become an animal ambassador for the purpose of wildlife education. Dorothy Lee has obtained all required permits from the State of Florida to care for and exhibit Trouper for educational purposes. On school and library visits Trouper is transported in a soft-sided carrier and placed in an enclosed playpen for display. He is gentle, healthy and a perfect animal ambassador.

The purpose of the *Trouper* series of books and presentations is to help children gain appreciation and respect for all animals and encourage them to share that knowledge with others. Forthcoming books in this series include:

Trouper's Teachings
Trouper Goes to the Beach
Holidays with Trouper
Trouper Goes to School
Trouper Goes to the Fire Station
Trouper Goes to the Police Station

THIS BOOK BELONGS TO

_____

The Beginning

This is Miss Dot. She worked as a *wildlife rehabilitator* and a teacher in the state of North Carolina.

She had special permission to take care of wild animals that were hurt, sick or left alone as babies.

She took them to her home and cared for them until they could go back to their natural environments, or homes, called *habitats*.

One summer afternoon a woman found a baby squirrel all alone. She called to ask if Miss Dot could take care of it. Miss Dot said she would come right over.

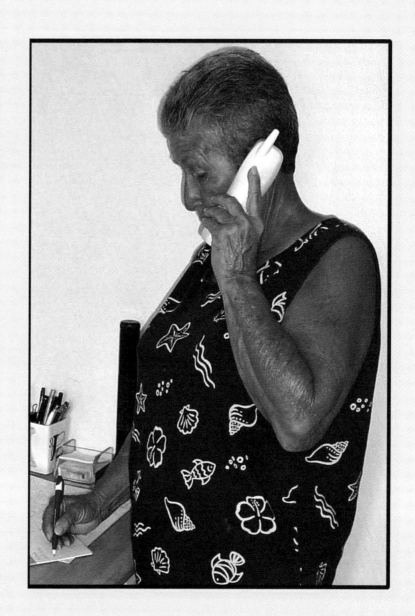

When she brought the baby squirrel home, two children ran up to ask Miss Dot what was inside the box.

She taught them all about squirrels. She knew the more the children learned about an animal, the more they would respect it.

She warned them, "Never pick up a wild animal, even if it can't move. It could hurt you or even make you sick. If you find an animal, and you are worried something is wrong with it, always tell an adult."

She took the baby squirrel inside and put it in a little cage where it would be safe.

Miss Dot received another phone call, this time from a friend. He had found an injured baby raccoon lying on its side in some tall grass on a golf course. He wanted Miss Dot to take care of it.

The little raccoon was only eight weeks old.

Baby raccoons are called *kits*. The injured kit didn't move and was bleeding from cuts on its head and nose.

Miss Dot took the kit home to help it. The little raccoon was very badly hurt.

She gave it water and medicine from a dropper because it couldn't open its mouth very well.

She put medicine on the raccoon's cuts to keep them from getting infected.

She cleaned the little kit and put it in a carrier with a soft blanket and a heating pad to keep it warm.

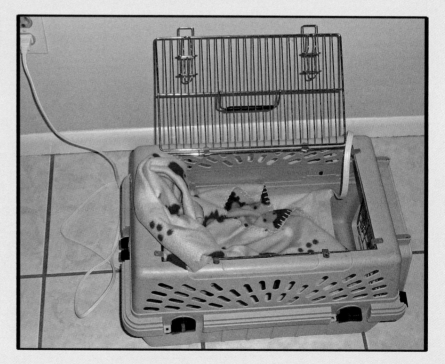

Day after day, Miss Dot was amazed the raccoon was still alive. Even after five days of loving care, the little raccoon still didn't move. All it did was breathe. Miss Dot believed it had *brain damage* from being hit on the head. She felt very sad because she thought it was going to die.

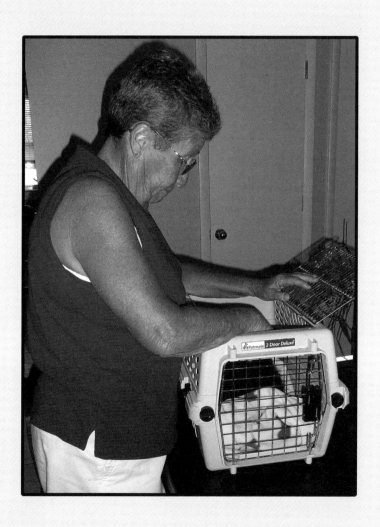

She looked into the carrier at the kit, and her tears dropped onto its fur.

"I'm so sorry, little one," she said. "I have done all I can for you, but you're not getting any better."

Just when she was about to give up, the baby raccoon picked up its head and yawned! It even moved its body a little bit.

Miss Dot was so happy!

"What a little trouper you are," she told the little kit.

A *trouper* is someone who goes through hard times without crying or complaining.

Then she gently picked him up and said, "I am going to name you *Trouper*."

She knew this little raccoon was fighting to live even though he was badly hurt.

He *was a real* trouper.

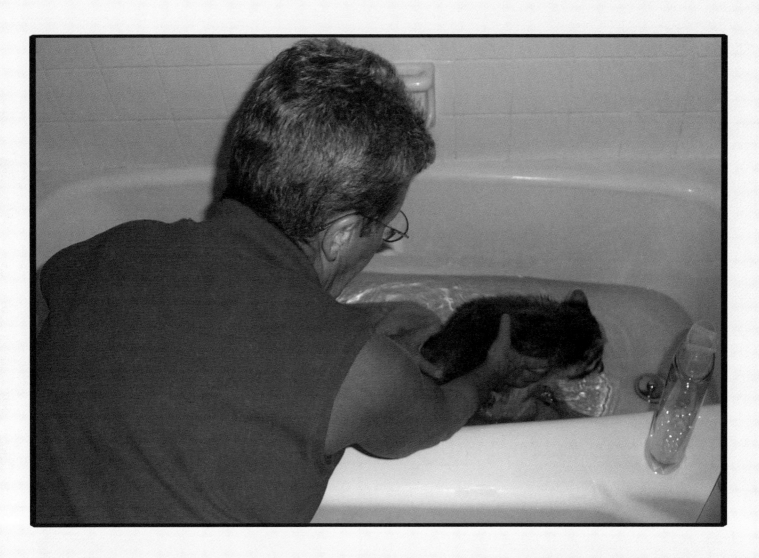

As Trouper got better, Miss Dot exercised him every day. She wanted his little body to get stronger and his wounds to heal. She carefully rubbed his muscles and moved his legs in warm water to help his body get well.

Trouper didn't seem
to mind the water at all,
even when he was given
a bath. As he got stronger,
he could almost stand
up without help by
leaning against the side
of the bathtub.

Miss Dot was very
proud of him.

After his bath one day, Miss Dot dried Trouper and looked into his eyes. He did not look back at her. She thought he might not be able to see.

She tested his eyes by shining a flashlight at his face. He didn't blink. He was *blind*.

Then she tested his hearing by clapping her hands next to his head. His ears didn't move. He was also *deaf*.

"Oh, no!" said Miss Dot. She was very upset. Trouper could never be set free if he couldn't hear or see.

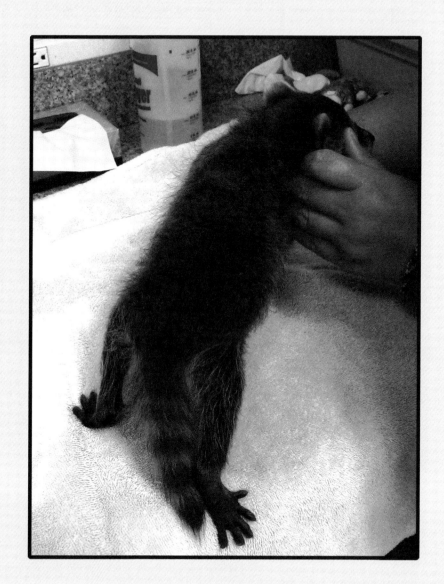

In North Carolina, if an animal couldn't go back into the wild, it had to be killed. That was the law. Miss Dot always obeyed the law, even if it hurt.

Miss Dot was worried that a *wildlife officer* would come and take Trouper away if he didn't get better.

She would not give up on Trouper. She believed he was getting better all the time. She hoped he would soon be able to see and hear her.

To exercise on his own, Miss Dot put Trouper in a soft playpen so he wouldn't hurt himself if he fell.

He practiced walking by feeling the sides of the playpen. It was a safe place for him, and he couldn't climb out.

Even though Trouper was improving, he still had problems.

Because his head was hurt, Trouper couldn't use his hands or eat by himself like other raccoons. Raccoons are famous for using their hands to feel food, especially in the water. Their little hands are human-like, with four fingers and a thumb. Some people believe they wash their food. They are really just feeling it and tearing at it to get the parts that can be eaten.

Miss Dot also worried that Trouper couldn't smell anything. When she put food in front of him, his little nose didn't move like it should have. But when food touched his tongue, he gobbled it up. There was no doubt that he could taste his food.

While getting well Trouper ate soft foods, like applesauce, smashed bananas and lemon pudding. He loved lemon pudding. He also liked baby human food, which was very good for him.

Several weeks later when Trouper was being fed next to Miss Dot, a storm came up. A boom of thunder shook the house. Trouper almost jumped into Miss Dot's lap.

"Oh, my goodness!" she said. "I think you can hear."

She put Trouper on the floor and clapped her hands near his ear. He turned his head toward the clapping sound. Miss Dot was so excited! Trouper's hearing had returned.

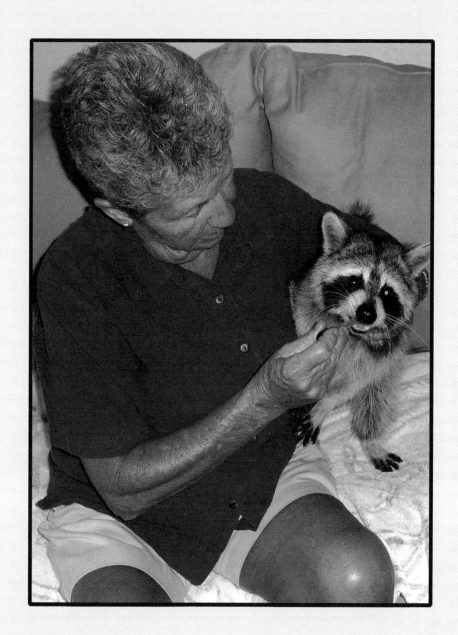

Because he was able to hear, Miss Dot started singing to him. She got close to his ear and sang a song she remembered from her childhood.

He seemed to enjoy it because he relaxed while she sang. After a while he made little raccoon noises back to her. It was like they were singing together.

14

Now Miss Dot felt good about taking Trouper outside to the back yard. He could follow her when he heard her sing. She even had a friend help her make up words for a song, just for Trouper.

Trouper's Song

Trouper is a little boy,
Trouper brings us lots of joy.
He is better than a toy,
Trouper is a little boy.

Trouper is a cute raccoon,
He was found in the month of June.
That is why we have this tune,
Trouper is a cute raccoon.

He was injured in the head,
He had to rest and heal in bed.
He was cared for and well fed,
"I LOVE YOU, Trouper," Miss Dot said.

"Trouper hears but cannot see,
That's okay 'cause he's with me.
He follows sound, and that's the key.

Now he has a family."

15

When Miss Dot stopped singing or making noises, Trouper walked in circles. That was because he couldn't see where he was going. He didn't know which way to turn.

Miss Dot started to sing again, and he walked straight toward her. Trouper followed her voice every time.

Trouper liked being outside as long as Miss Dot was with him.

They went for walks along the backyard fence. Trouper could feel the grass under his hands, as well as little rocks and leaves. He couldn't pick them up like other raccoons do, but he did stop to feel things on the ground.

If he walked into a puddle, he would press his hands down into it. Raccoons have sensitive hands and they often feel around in the water for things to grab.

After six months, Trouper had made great progress. He could hear, eat more solid foods, go for walks and feel things with his hands. But, he still couldn't see, smell anything or feed himself. He would never be set free.

Miss Dot was worried. If she stayed in North Carolina, Trouper would be taken away. She had a big decision to make.

The only other thing she could do was move to a place where Trouper would be safe. Miss Dot picked three states on a map and looked up their laws on keeping wild animals.

She studied each state's laws and then knew exactly where they could go — Florida!

Florida is where Trouper could finally be safe at home. By getting a special Florida permit, Miss Dot could keep Trouper.

Florida

It was time to pack up their things and move to their new home.

Trouper made sure his lemon pudding was packed, too.

The drive to Florida from North Carolina took two days. When they arrived at their new home in Fort Myers, Florida, Miss Dot gave Trouper his own bedroom.

He was free to go out in public where other pets were welcome.

Once they were settled
into their new home,
Miss Dot made a plan.
The first thing she did
was get the Florida
permit to keep Trouper.
By getting a permit, she
agreed to take good
care of him. She prom-
ised she would keep
him safe and healthy.
She loved Trouper.

Miss Dot wanted to save and help all animals, so she found a local *wildlife hospital* where she could help. The hospital was called CROW, which stands for **C**linic for the **R**ehabilitation **o**f **W**ildlife. CROW is one of the oldest wildlife hospitals in the United States of America.

They were happy to have Miss Dot's help. She took injured animals to the hospital, cleaned cages, and she loved to feed the orphaned baby animals. An *orphan* has no parents.

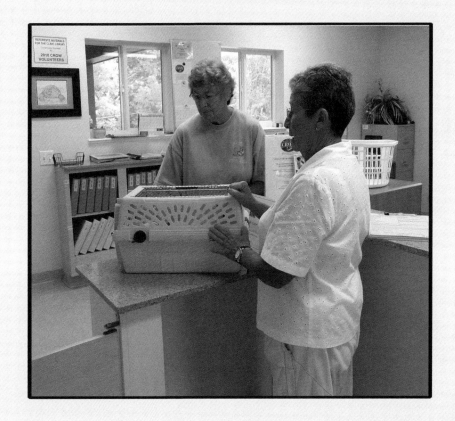

Miss Dot wanted Trouper's story told in a book. She went to a bookstore to find an author to help her. An *author* is a person who writes stories for books.

At the bookstore Miss Dot found some children's books about wildlife. One book's author, Kyle Miller, lived nearby. Miss Dot decided to give her a call.

She learned that Kyle Miller was also a volunteer at CROW. She loved to teach about wildlife. She agreed that it was important to tell Trouper's story. Miss Dot and Kyle Miller talked about how they could tell Trouper's story.

They thought it would be a good idea to write a book. They also wanted to create an *educational program* so children could learn about respecting and protecting wildlife.

The most exciting part of the program was that they could take Trouper with them.

Miss Dot wanted Trouper to become an *animal ambassador*. That meant he would be a living example of the good side and the bad side of how people treat wildlife.

FOR KIDS

When you come upon a wild animal that appears to be hurt you should always ...

 Slowly back up and never touch the animal.

 Tell an adult like a parent, guardian, policeman, or fireman so they can . . .

 Observe the animal to decide if it needs help or not - the adult will make the . . .

 Phone call to the appropriate rescue service.

Part of Miss Dot's teaching is a S.T.O.P. sign for children. STOP is what children should do when they come upon a sick or injured wild animal. The reason for the STOP sign is to keep kids from getting bitten or sick and to get help for the animal. The STOP sign reminds them what each letter stands for:

S is a snake   —Slowly back up.

T is a turtle   —Tell an adult.

O is an owl   — Observe or watch the animal.

P is a panther —Phone the rescue service.

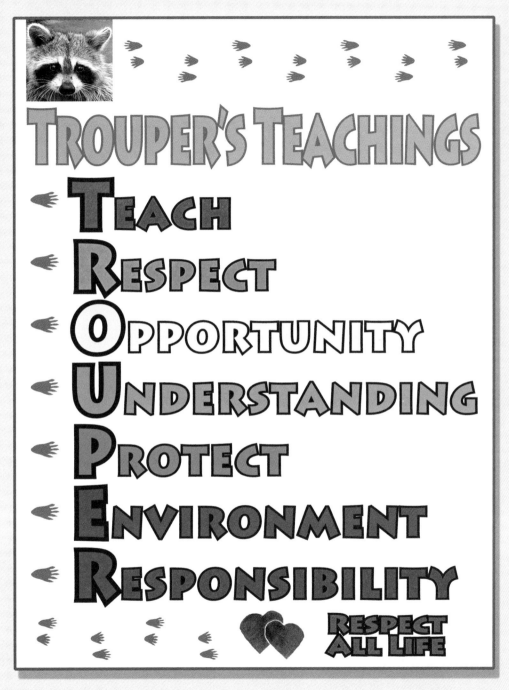

TROUPER'S TEACHINGS:

Teach people to

Respect animals at every

Opportunity so they

Understand that

Protecting animals and our

Environment is necessary for the future of wildlife, and each of has a

Responsibility for what we do and say. In this way we show that we respect all life.

Teach —

Everything you do is teaching. If you are kind to animals you are teaching others, by example, to be kind to animals. If you are mean to animals, you are teaching others to be mean to animals.

Everything you say is teaching. If you say, "I like animals," you are teaching others to like animals. If you say, "That animal is no good," you are teaching others to see animals as no good.

What other ways can you teach about animals?

Respect —

Respect for an animal means you have positive feelings for it. If an animal tries to bite you, you understand it is acting naturally or it is afraid. So you treat it with respect by staying away from it. Then you can enjoy it from a safe distance.

What other ways can you show respect for animals?

Opportunity —

Very often you have a chance, or opportunity, to teach respect for animals. You might see an animal outdoors, on the TV or in a picture. Then you can talk about that animal in a positive way. Every day there are opportunities to teach respect for animals.

What other opportunities do you have to teach respect for animals?

28

Understanding —

The more you understand or know about animals the more you will respect them. You understand animals better when you watch them in the wild, read about them, watch nature videos, and listen to teachers.

What other ways can you think of to understand animals?

Protect —

You protect animals by teaching others to respect and understand them. You protect them from harm by keeping them safe. You protect them by preventing destruction of their homes and habitat.

What other ways can you think of to protect animals?

Environment —

An environment is the place where animals live. It is their habitat or home. It is a place where they raise their young. It can be anywhere and we hope it is a safe place.

What ways can you think of to keep animals' homes safe?

Responsibility —

Being responsible is taking responsibility for what we say and do. It means that we choose what we say and choose what we do that helps protect all wildlife.

What ways can you choose to be responsible for wildlife?

Trouper's Teachings

When you choose to teach respect for animals at every opportunity it will help people understand that we need to protect them and their environment. This happens when you take responsibility for your actions. When you learn to respect animals, you learn to **respect all life.**

"The greatness of a nation and its moral progress can be judged by the way its animals are treated."
Mahatma Gandhi

More For Parents

This book is just The Beginning of Trouper's adventures. As an ambassador animal he will continue to visit schools, libraries, wildlife educational centers, fairs, festivals, birthday parties and more. He will be presented to groups or organizations interested in learning about promoting the welfare and protection of wildlife and their habitats enjoyed by so many. As children learn to respect and protect animals they are more likely to respect and protect each other.

We invite you to visit Trouper's website, **www.trouperraccoon.com**, and his facebook page, **Trouper Lee**, and **Trouper Raccoon** on Twitter, to keep up with his activities.

We invite all children to become a Trouper's Teacher and tell their friends and family all about respecting and protecting wildlife. Children who come to a Trouper program can earn an official Trouper's Teacher certificate along with a photo of Trouper, signed by Trouper's hand.

Enjoy raccoon facts, resources and Trouper's pictures on the next pages. Most of the photos were taken in the Fort Myers and Sanibel Island, Florida area.

Raccoon Facts

Raccoons are known to carry *rabies*, a deadly disease they spread by biting other animals or people.

Raccoons can weigh 12 to 48 pounds.

Raccoons can use their fingers to turn doorknobs, open refrigerators, get into garbage cans and get into trouble.

The word raccoon comes from an Algonquin Indian word, aroughcoune, meaning "he scratches with his hands." Raccoons use their hands to feel for food in the water.

Although captive raccoons have been known to live over twenty years, they live in the wild only two to three years. In many areas hunting and traffic accidents are the two most common causes of death.

Raccoons build dens in trees, the eaves of houses, attics, cars and in hollow logs.

Raccoons are mostly *nocturnal*, except in coastal Florida when, during the day, they hunt for food with the tides. Nocturnal means they are active at night.

Raccoons eat plants, such as grapes, nuts and berries. They also eat insects, including grubs, grasshoppers and crickets. Sometimes raccoons will eat voles, deer mice, squirrels and other small mammals. They will enjoy bird's eggs and nestlings. When near water they like to eat small fish, shrimp and shell fish. A mammal is a warm-blooded animal that feeds its newborn young with milk. A nestling is a baby bird that is unable to fly from its nest.

A Day in the life of Trouper the blind raccoon

Good morning!

Where's breakfast!

Potty first

Yummy, breakfast!

Stretching exercises

Getting nails trimmed

Let's go out and play!

I love listening to music!

Time for a nap

Mommy, where are you!

I love my Mom.

Trouper's Fun Days

Going to the beach, yippee!

Oh, the water is warm

Look! I'm swimming!

Mom's always there for me

Uh Oh! Get my leash!

I make a great dancing partner!

Shhh, I'm hiding

After bath, I'm tired

Great day! Sweet dreams!

About Miss Dot and Kyle Miller

Dorothy Lee became a wildlife rehabilitator after she retired from teaching Special Education in middle school in North Carolina. She relocated to Southwest Florida in 2010 with Trouper the blind raccoon. She then became a volunteer at C.R.O.W., the Clinic for the Rehabilitation of Wildlife, and became involved in wildlife education programs.

Miss Dot stays busy giving educational talks about her experiences as a wildlife rehabilitator, everything she knows about raccoons and her life with Trouper. She often takes Trouper as an animal ambassador to schools, libraries, wildlife centers and organized groups.

Miss Dot can be reached at (239) 482-7176, trouperlee2011@aol.com, **www.trouperraccoon.com**

Dorothy Lee

Kyle L. Miller is an award winning author, publisher and wildlife educator. She retired from teaching and coaching in the Northeast to Sanibel Island, FL in 1999. She founded Jungle House Publications and in 2005 published her first award-winning wildlife storybook for children, *DILLO — A Baby Armadillo's Adventure on Sanibel Island*. Kyle's second award winning book, *Snowy Pea and the Ghost Crab*, was published in 2011. Her passion for wildlife and teaching is at the heart of her writing.

Kyle conducts educational presentations based on her books and has joined Miss Dot with talks about Trouper and his life adventures. She has a MS degree in Physical Education and a MA degree in Counseling Psychology. She is Vice President and Treasurer of the Florida Publishers Association, and she is a member of the Independent Book Publishers Association and the Gulf Coast Writer's Association.

Kyle can be reached at (239) 472-0599, kmiller765@aol.com, junglehousepub@yahoo.com, **www.junglehousepublications.com.**

Kyle L. Miller

Websites For Kids

The following websites are fun, educational and loaded with interesting information about raccoons, and wildlife in general, for kids. There are many more websites featuring raccoons and wildlife that might be fun for kids to discover. Ask your parents or a librarian to help you find more information.

PAWS — paws.org/kids-raccoons.html

Paws is a website at which kids can find a lot of information about a variety of animals, including raccoons.

Department of Natural Resources — Wisconsin

dnr.state.wi.us/org/caer/ce/eek/index.htm

dnr.state.wi.us/eek/critter/mammal/raccoon.htm

Environmental Education for Kids — EEK! is an electronic magazine for kids 4-8 that features information and fun activities in the great outdoors.

Kids Planet — Defenders of Wildlife — kidsplanet.org

defenders.org/index_v2.html

Kids Planet is produced by Defenders of Wildlife and is packed with information about wildlife, and features games and activities.

Best Wildlife Websites for Kids — Countryfile.com

countryfile.com/countryside/best-wildlife-websites-kids

This is a great resource, offering a number of wildlife websites for kids, full of facts and fun activities.

Wildlife Kids Club — by the Wildlife Associates

wildlifekidsclub.org/main/index.php

Wildlife Especially for Kids — from the U.S. Fish and Wildlife Service — fws.gov/kids

This site is loaded with information about wildlife, especially for kids.

The following websites have books specifically about raccoons from picture books to chapter books for children:

www.books.google.com/books?id=vnhVibvnzvIC&dq=isbn:0774809647

www.first-school.ws/activities/books/animals/wild/raccoon-picture-book.htm

www.amazon.com

Glossary

animal ambassador — An animal that cannot be released into its natural habitat because of injury. It is often used for wildlife educational purposes. Animal ambassadors help establish a connection between people and the natural world of animals.

author — A person who creates and writes a book or other written works.

blind — An animal or person that cannot see.

brain damage — An injury to the brain that can affect the senses (feeling, seeing, hearing, tasting, smelling), as well as movement and thoughts.

deaf — An animal or person that cannot hear.

den — The hidden home of a wild animal.

educational program — Teaching about something, like wild animals, that takes place in a classroom, libraries, or other places where teaching takes place.

environment — The natural world where people, animals and plants live.

habitat — A place in nature where animals live and raise their young.

kit — The name for a baby raccoon. More than one kit are kittens.

permit — Official permission for a person or group to own something or do something.

nocturnal — Active and feeding at night more than during the day.

mammal — A mammal produces milk to feed its babies. It has hair. Its lower jaw is a single bone on either side. It has a special muscle that separates its stomach area from its lungs.

nestling — A young bird that doesn't yet have its feathers for flying and cannot leave the nest.

opportunity — A chance to do something

orphan — An animal or child without parents.

rabies — A sickness that causes death in animals. If bitten by an animal with rabies humans can die if not treated with medicine right away. Raccoons, foxes, skunks, coyotes, dogs and cats can carry rabies.

respect — Feeling good or positive about something or someone.

responsible — Making decisions about what to do or say can make things better or worse. Always try to be responsible and make good decisions.

Trouper's Teachings — A set of words that start with the letters in Trouper's name. The words are: Teach, Respect, Opportunity, Understanding, Protect, Environment, and Responsibility. Trouper's Teachings tell important ways to help protect animals and their homes from harm.

Trouper vs. Trooper — A Trouper is someone who goes through hard times without crying or complaining. A Trooper is a policeman or police woman or soldier.

veterinarian — An animal doctor.

wildlife hospital — A place where sick, injured or orphaned wild animals are taken to be treated by animal doctors, or veterinarians. **Hopefully,** these animals are brought back to good health and returned to their natural environment.

wildlife officer — A person who makes sure wildlife laws are followed.

wildlife rehabilitator — A person who is permitted by law to rescue, care for and return sick, injured or orphan animals back to good health so they can be released into the wild.

Now let's see what you have learned!
What do each of the letters below stand for?
Write your answer on the line next to the letter.

S _____

T _____

O _____

P _____

What do the letters below mean?
Write your answer on the line next to the letter.

T

R

O

U

P

E

R

39

What five ways can you help protect wild animals?

1. _____

2. _____

3. _____

4. _____

5. _____

Write a short story about your favorite wild animal.

_____

_____

_____

_____

_____

_____

_____

What are your three favorite animals and why should people respect them?

_____

_____

_____

_____

_____

_____

_____

This sample of a Certificate of Accomplishment is awarded to anyone who completes the educational requirements to become a Trouper's Teacher. The educational requirements are to read this book and answer all the questions on pages 38 through 42.
You may send your answers on-line to: trouperlee2011@aol.com or by mail to:
    Trouper's Teacher Certificate, P.O. Box 481, Sanibel, FL 33957.

TROUPER'S TEACHER

this certifies that

Your name goes here!
_____

has successfully completed the required course of study approved by the Trouper's Teachings Education Department and is therefore awarded this

CERTIFICATE OF ACCOMPLISHMENT

Given this _____ day of _____ 20 _____

_____   _____
Department Supervisor   Head of Department

Is that my song?